WOULD YOU RATHER & TRUTH OR DARE

Interactive Game Book For Kids, Family And Friends

Hilarious Jokes, Silly Scenarios And Challenging Choises

DEDICATION

This book is dedicated to all children and to all people who never stop dreaming, learning and trying to change their own and our future, word after word, idea after idea...

DIGITAL BOOKS

Disclaimer Notice:

Please note the information contained within this document is for educational and entertainment purposes only. All effort has been executed to present accurate, up to date, and reliable, complete information. No warranties of any kind are declared or implied. Readers acknowledge that the author is not engaging in the rendering of legal, financial, medical or professional advice. The content within this book has been derived from various sources. Please consult a licensed professional before attempting any techniques outlined in this book.

By reading this document, the reader agrees that under no circumstances is the author responsible for any losses, direct or indirect, which are incurred as a result of the use of the information contained within this document, including, but not limited to, — errors, omissions, or inaccuracies.

I Little Request For You...

Dear Valued Customer,

We're A Small Publishing Company And Without **Your Support** We Would Not Exist.

Therefore, We Make A Humble Request, If You Enjoy This Book, Please Spare A Few Minutes To Leave Us A Review On Amazon Book Product Page.

Each And Every One Of Your Reviews If **Very Important** To Us And Can Help Us To Compete Against Larger Corporations And Their Bigger Marketing Budgets.

We're Forever Grateful For Your Support And We Hope We've Succeeded In Providing You Or Your Loved One With A Very Special Book.

Sincerly,

Table of Contents

PART I: WOULD YOU RATHER

Instructions for 'Would You Rather' Game book For Family and Friends.

'Would you rather ride an ostrich or a zebra?'

'Would you rather dance with a grumpy old troll or a hungry giant?'

Are you sure you know what answers to pick for your friends or family? Well if you don't, here's a chance to find out through these silly and hilarious questions lined up for you and your amazing family. Spending a little time to hear and laugh at each others answers or reactions will be worth it and will create a cozy family mood.

The different sections of the book help you and your family explore various aspects of characters and the funniest ideals or opinions on things you probably haven't ever imagined before. From funny situations, love and friendship or places round the world, to embarrassing truths, gross or strange foods and magical mysteries, let the fun take you over!

Instructions: Roll up papers with numbers 1 to 30 written on them. Everyone gets to pick a paper, and then they answer the question attached to the number. Five marks for answering each question. The person who can answer the most questions wins. If the cringe factor is too high for someone and they can't pick between the two hilarious options provided, then they lose points. Pick a crazy option and win points!

This game contains many different and entertaining sections which include:

- Would You Rather - Pets : Random, Save The Pets, and Pretty Big and Pretty Small.

- Would You Rather - Monsters and Ghosts, Magical Places, Beasts and Beauties : Random, Spirited Away, and Superhero Powers.

- Would You Rather - Amazing Animals and Interesting Insects: Random, Animal and Insect Instincts, Cute and Cuddly Factor.

- Would You Rather - Embarrassing Moments! : Random, Crush Nightmare, and Friend Fails.

- Would You Rather - Beauty? Or Not? : Random, Social Statements, Fashion Fails or Finesse?

- Would You Rather - Food : Random, Crazy Combinations and Lets Get Exotic!

- Would You Rather - Love and Friendship : Random, Crush Country and Celebrity City.

- Would You Rather - Technology & Social Media : Random, Social Media Situations.

- Would You Rather - Luxury & Riches, Travel & Leisure : Random, Exciting Events and Travel Train.

- Would You Rather - Sports and Exercises : Random, Sweetest Exercises and Energetic Sports.

- Would You Rather - World Changers : Random, Careers & Legends.

- **BONUS SEGMENT**: Babysitter's Trouble! : Random & Dirty Diapers. (55 questions only

Chapter 1: Would You Rather – Pets

Random:

All the choices to make from every perspective. This section is as unpredictable as our lovely and charismatic pets. How much can we tolerate?

1. Would you rather brush the fur of your very grumpy cat or chase your dog around to give it a bath?

2. Would you rather own a wild , wild chihuahua that attacks all your friends or a bad tempered snake that escapes from its cage once in a while.

3. Would you rather get pecked hard by your really annoyed parrot, or have your pet pigeons eat and spill your entire breakfast?

4. Would you rather have your pet pony follow you all the way to school without you knowing, or a pet pig that sneaks into your parent's car and follows them to work (they don't find out until they're at work) ?

5. Would you rather have your cat pee all over your clothes, or dog vomit all over your favorite snack?

6. Would you rather own a million cats or a million snakes?

7. Would you rather get tormented by your pet tarantula who likes to crawl into your shirt all the time, or your pet lizard that somehow gets into your clothes and startles you most of the time?

8. Would you rather have a pitbull that bullies everyone when they're eating, or a stubborn billy goat that eats most of the cushions in your house?

9. Would you rather live with your pet rabbits and a wolf, or Siamese cats and a puppy?

10. Would you rather go to a cat show with a dog, or a dog show with a cat?

11. Would you rather dye your pet or have to dress it up in clothes?

12. Would you rather own a pet alligator that snaps at anyone that comes near it, or a parrot that tells everyone 'Come closer, and I'll peck your eyeballs out!"

13. Would you rather let your pet drive your car or let it barb your hair?

14. Would you rather have your pet poop on your brand new clothes or pee in someone's car?

15. Would you rather have a super smart pet or an extremely amusing and talented one?

16. Would you rather have a pet that can walk the tightrope or a pet that can call the police?

17. Would you rather have a pet that attacks other people's pets all the time or one that bites people all the time?

18. Would you rather eat dog food with a dog or eat cat food with a cat?

19. Would you rather have a timid pet that is really adorable, or a very smart pet but very rough looking and always dirty?

20. Would you rather have a pet that always pees in a crowded place in public, or a well behaved pet that doesn't want to play with anyone but you?

21. Would you rather never have children or never have pets?

22. Would you rather own a pet mini goat or own a fox?

23. Would you rather be allergic to animals or get tired of them easily?

24. Would you rather have your pet bite your hand or bite your leg?

25. Would you rather be the cat pet of a wealthy family or have a dog and take care of it all the time?

26. Would you rather be stuck in a place with a hundred bunnies or swim in an aquarium with many goldfish?

27. Would you rather have a pug or a French bull dog?

28. Would you rather curl up with a Pomeranian or a Daschund?

29. Would you rather carry your dog like a backpack always or run after your dog always?

30. Would you rather have a dog that always smells like poop or a dog that always smells like sprayed skunk?

Save The Pets!

What can you do just to save a pet? What pet would you pick over another to save? Guess we'll find out!

31. Would you rather save a cat from a fire or a dog from drowning?

32. Would you rather save mice from a cat or a cat from a group of dogs?

33. Would you rather save a pet pig from a wolf or an elephant from hunters?

34. Would you rather save your pet hamster from a fox trying to bite it or some rabbits from a fox trying to eat them?

35. Would you rather save your pet chicken from a crazy cook or your pet goat from a crazy cook?

36. Would you rather save your pet dog by not letting it eat chocolate which can kill it, or save your cat from getting attacked by the dog by not allowing it to torment the dog?

37. Would you rather save your pet shark from a group of crazy piranhas or your pet monkey from a group of mad gorillas?

38. Would you rather save your domesticated tiger from other wild tigers or save your pet lion from wild lions in the wild?

39. Would you rather save your parrots from a hungry cat or save your naughty lemurs from an angry neighbor whose house they ruined.

40. Would you rather save a chihuahua and let your favorite shirt be ruined or save a pitbull and let your favorite jeans get ruined?

41. Would you rather save your pet lizards from a cat or stop a death fight between a pet cobra and pet scorpion?

42. Would you rather save your pet cow from getting used for meat or a group of pet birds from being used for barbecue bird meat?

43. Would you rather save ten tiny chimps from a large wolfdog, or save a large wolfdog from a thousand lobsters?

44. Would you rather save a bear from a large baboon or a sloth from ten ferrets?
45.. Would you rather save flies from a frog or pet centipedes from lizards?

46. Would you rather save pet bugs from a lemur or save lemurs from finger monkeys?

47. Would you rather save pet fish from getting eaten by pet polar bears, or save pet polar bears from hunters?

48. Would you rather save reindeer from bloodthirsty hyenas or save deer from a group of bloodthirsty hyenas?

49. Would you rather save your tiny goldfish from getting killed in their bowl or swim after a large goldfish in a river?

50. Would you rather save your pet lion from your pet tiger or your pet tiger from your pet lion?

Pretty Big or Pretty Small?

From an elephant to mice, pets of all sizes are lined up for you in this segment. Find out how big your heart is, and what courage, to own a giant pet or a tiny one.

51. Would you rather own a 43 inch tall Great Dane or ten rats?

52. Would you rather own a 30 pound cat or a fox?

53. Would you rather own a 15 inch long goldfish or a tiny leopard gecko?

54. Would you rather own a roborovoski dwarf hamster or a large horse?

55. Would you rather own a thousand rabbits or a 115 pound tortoise?

56. Would you rather own twenty small parrots or a large donkey that is 5 feet and 8 inches in height?

57. Would you rather own a 1 foot, 1.3 inches big and large hamster or fifty guinea pigs?

58. Would you rather own twenty mischievous ferrets or a 55 pound rabbit ?

59. Would you rather own a million betta fish that are a few inches or a 140 pound capybara?

60. Would you rather own a 'bearded dragon' that is two feet long or five thousand tree frogs?

61. Would you rather own twenty tarantulas or a wallaby, which is big, and almost like a mini kangaroo?

62. Would you rather own a chimp that is 150 pounds or ten small box turtles that live up to 40 years?

63. Would you rather own ten chinchillas or a hyacinth macaw that is 40 inches tall and has a 60 inch wingspan?

64. Would you rather own a ball python that is three or four feet long or ten hermit crabs?

65. Would you rather own fifteen gerbils or a large pot bellied pig?

66. Would you rather own two hundred hedgehogs or a wolf?

67. Would you rather own a lion or a thousand sugar gliders?

68. Would you rather own five thousand brine shrimp or a tiger?

69. Would you rather own a large sloth or fifteen wolfdogs?

70. Would you rather own twenty cobra snakes or two grown polar bears?

71. Would you rather own ten marmosets or a hippopotamus?

72. Would you rather a large alligator or fifty Madagascar Hissing Cockroaches?

73. Would you rather own thirty wolfdogs or three boa constrictor snakes?

74. Would you rather own three big elephants or six lemurs?

75. Would you rather own twenty scorpions or three large Llamas?

76. Would you rather have ten finger monkeys or ten reindeer?

77. Would you rather own fifteen hyenas or five miniature donkeys?

78. Would you rather own ten kinkajou (small, smart and sly pets that are hard to tame) or one giant Anteater (which is likely to go wild and attack).

79. Would you rather own a great white shark or twenty pygmy goats?

80. Would you rather have thirty bush babies as pets or ten hyenas?

Chapter 2: Would You Rather - Monsters and Ghosts, Magical Places, Beasts and Beauties.

Random:

Have magical adventures or journeys, with fearful, beautiful, ancient or beastly magical creatures. Get transported or transformed when you make your choice. A swish from a magic wand, and we begin!

1. Would you rather go to a fairy party and ride dragonflies, or go to an imps meeting and steal gold from an evil imp?

2. Would you rather engage in a battle with giants or a fight with five cyclops (giants too, but with only one eye)?

3. Would you rather save a ship from sirens, or team up with mermaids to destroy a pirate ship?

4. Would you rather have ears like an elf or big feet like an imp?

5. Would you rather be as mischievous as a pixie or as naughty as an elf?

6. Would you rather be turned to ice by an ice dragon or fried to a crisp by the hot fiery breath of a fire dragon?

7. Would you rather be changed into an ugly, wicked witch always traveling with a broom, or be transformed into an ogre, and scare people or maybe even eat them?

8. Would you rather fight the Loch Ness monster with a team of sailors or a giant squid with a million divers?

9. Would you rather use a shield and sword to fight a basilisk or have a no weapons fight with a vampire?

10. Would you rather become a hairy strong werewolf or be a centaur with horse legs and half of a human body?

11. Would you rather be a genie in a bottle, trapped for eighty years, or be a siren bound to a curse, never to be human until after eighty years as well?

12. Would you rather get into a staring contest with a gorgon or get into a maze with a bloodthirsty minotaur?

13. Would you rather be a servant to an evil wizard, or host parties for bunches of wicked witches?

14. Would you rather play a game of riddles to cross a troll's bridge and risk getting eaten, or answer riddles from a sphinx and also risk getting eaten?

15. Would you rather have snakes as hair, like Medusa, or be one of three old witches who share only an eye?

16. Would you rather get swallowed by a sea that has a wide gaping mouth and a human face form, or stomped on by a group of magical mountains shaped like large stone soldiers?

17. Would you rather become a living tree with branches growing out of your mouth, or become a fearful river, full of sea life, that takes your human form when you please?

18. Would you rather get kidnapped by fairies as their slave for as long as they please or be forced to run errands for imps thrice every week?

19. Would you rather get your insides torn apart by a wild banshee or be tormented by a really scary ghost until you are frightened beyond sanity?

20. Would you rather camp with the legendary bigfoot for a year or live with Frankenstein and his bad temper for three months?

21. Would you rather get trapped in a magical book full of magical beasts and scary stories and find your own way out, OR

get carried away by a whirlwind and find yourself caught in a battle between the Wicked Witch of the West and her flying monkeys?

22. Would you rather save a princess from a tower with a fearful dragon, or fight a princess who turns to a living, bloodthirsty gargoyle at night?

23. Would you rather live in a house full of angry ghosts, or be forced to entertain a group of demons who intend to have you for dinner afterwards?

24. Would you rather be a dryad and live out a long existence as part of a tree, or a magical sea serpent that survives only as long as it is within the sea?

25. Would you rather fight a group of zombies or get through a jungle full of man eating plants?

26. Would you rather be chased down a lonely bridge by midnight, by a headless ghost or have a group of ghosts covered in blood by your bedside every night, just staring at you?

27. Would you rather fetch water from a well with a vengeful ghost in it, or eat at a table where all the plates, knives and forks are used to attack you, by an invincible force?

28. Would you rather spend time in Dracula's castle and risk getting whisked away any day and any time by the vanishing

castle, or participate in a school play where you get harassed by the Phantom of the Opera ghost and nobody can see the ghost but you?

29. Would you rather try to overthrow Zeus, greatest of the Greek gods or fight the god of War?

30. Would you rather get hit by a magical comet or lasered down through the fire shooting eyes of a fire dragon?

31. Would you rather hear the voices of ghouls at night or see some strange and scary masquerades by your bed in the middle of the night?

32. Would you rather be a witch hunter or be a vampire hunter?

33. Would you rather have the magical ability to talk to animals or the magical ability to speak all the languages in the world?

34. Would you rather be a superhero with useless powers or a magical being that just absorbs magic but can't use it?

35. Would you rather be able to blast people with stones or be able to hit them with trees?

36. Would you rather be a leprechaun or be a dwarf?

37. Would you rather have the ability to stop wars or the ability to stop natural disasters?

38. Would you rather have the power to turn things pink or turn things blue?

39. Would you rather have the ability to start water fountains or create rose gardens?

40. Would you rather have the ability to start a thunderstorm or the ability to start a hailstorm?

Spirited Away:

Magical beings can really cast all sorts of spells! Can you choose a magical place you'd prefer to be spirited away to? It is either one enchantment or the other! And now, the magic begins!

41. Would you rather be spirited away to Nysa, a beautiful valley in Greek mythology or Alfheim, a land of elves?

42. Would you rather be spirited away to Agartha, a legendary city at earth's core or Asgard, the city of the gods built by Odin?

43. Would you rather be spirited away to Avalon, the final resting place of King Arthur or Camelot, King Arthur's city?

44. Would you rather be spirited away to Magic Road, Waterford, or Fairyland?

45. Would you rather be spirited away to Atlantis or Axis Mundi, rumored to be the center of the world, or connection between heaven and earth?

46. Would you rather be spirited away to Feather Mountain, a mythological Mountain in Chinese mythology or Garden of the Hesperides, sacred garden of Hera, from where the gods got their immortality?

47. Would you rather be spirited away to Hel, an Underworld in Norse Mythology or the Kingdom of Saguenay, a kingdom full of blond rich people?

48. Would you rather be spirited away to Lemuria, a lost land or Olympus, home of the twelve Olympian gods?

49. Would you rather be spirited away to Arcadia, a peaceful land that's like a vision or Baptist, Island of Amber?

50. Would you rather be spirited away to Cloud Cukoo land which is situated within the clouds or Cockaigne, a legendary land where no want exists?

Superhero Powers:

Choose between two great powers or two useless ones! A funny power or a totally annoying one. One power from each question has to be your choice!

51. Would you rather have x-ray vision or super hearing?

52. Would you rather be able to read minds or see the future?

53. Would you rather be able to teleport or time travel?

54. Would you rather have the power to make every season summer or the power to make every season winter?

55. Would you rather be able to turn everything to ice or the power to burn everything?

56. Would you rather have the power to bend forks or the power to break dishes?

57. Would you rather have the power to read minds or the power to control people's bodies?

58. Would you rather have the power to change the TV channel without the remote or the power to get your phone to just play any song you like without having to get any one?

59. Would you rather have the power to change your hair into any color you like or change your clothes into any color you like?

60. Would you rather have the ability to change anything to gold or the power to change anything to diamonds?

61. Would you rather have the power to get any food you want at any time to appear before you or have the ability to get free browsing data or WiFi wherever you are and whenever you want?

62. Would you rather have the power to gain all the knowledge in the world or the power to be and retain the position of the most powerful person in the world?

63. Would you rather have the power to make anyone fall in love with you or the power to make people give you anything you want?

64. Would you rather have the power to use your fart to fly or have the power to melt things with vomit?

65. Would you rather have the power to make people keep quiet or the power to make a person talk until their jaws drop off?

66. Would you rather have the power to create glitter out of nowhere or the power to make colored marbles out of nowhere?

67. Would you rather have the power to make butterflies appear out of anywhere or the power to make exotic birds appear out of anywhere?

68. Would you rather have the power to control water or the power to control wind?

69. Would you rather have the power to live underwater like a fish or the power to fly?

70. Would you rather have the ability to understand dogs or the ability to understand cats?

71. Would you rather have the ability to make anyone dance or the ability to make anyone sing?

72. Would you rather have the power to create cute pets or the power to create pretty flowers?

73. Would you rather have the power to turn people's heads to fish heads or the power to make a person look like a bat?

74. Would you rather have the power to make places smell nice or the power to neutralize bad odors?

75. Would you rather have the power to heal others or the power to heal yourself no matter what injury you have?

76. Would you rather have the ability to turn a place into the desert or into a rainforest if you like?

77. Would you rather have the ability to scare people so badly that they melt or the ability to make people walk until they turn to skeletons?

78. Would you rather have the power to make dying plants grow again or the ability to make dying animals recuperate?

79. Would you rather have the power to have magical beings do your chores or homework or responsibilities or have the power to do any sport you like perfectly?

80. Would you rather have the ability to cause heavy rainfall or strong winds?

Chap 3: Would You Rather - Amazing Animals and Interesting Insects!

Random:

Things can get crazy in the wild really quickly. What bizarre situation can you 'bear' with animals? What choices can be made?

1. Would you rather eat with a hungry chimpanzee or run off with a panda's dinner?

2. Would you rather eat roasted tarantulas or fried grasshoppers?

3. Would you rather chase an antelope or have a race against a deer?

4. Would you rather swim like a dolphin or fly like an eagle?

5. Would you rather have a long neck like a giraffe, to look at everyone from above, or a trunk like an elephant, to splash water all over unsuspecting people?

6. Would you rather eat grass like a cow, or slop from a trough like a pig?

7. Would you rather neigh like a horse, or quack like a duck?

8. Would you rather be a swan in a beautiful pond, or a flamingo in a tropical paradise?

9. Would you rather have the ability to jump like a rabbit, or flutter like a butterfly?

10. Would you rather be able to talk like a parrot, or sing sweet tunes like a songbird?

11. Would you rather get chased by a turkey or punched hard in the stomach by a kangaroo?

12. Would you rather have centipedes squirming around in your shirt or worms in your hair?

13. Would you rather swim off with a crocodile's lunch and risk it chasing you or ride on a lion's back and hope not to be thrown off?

14. Would you rather be spiked by a porcupine, or sprayed with smelly fluid from a skunk?

15. Would you rather be a chicken in a farm and risk getting eaten or be a bear in a hunting region, during hunting season, and risk getting shot at or caught by hunting dogs?

16. Would you rather have a seagull steal your shiny new watch or a group of squirrels swoop down on your food during a picnic and run off with all of it?

17. Would you rather go into a bat cave with a lot of carnivorous bats that are likely to attack, or be stuck in a cage with a tiger and its newborn cubs?

18. Would you rather be made fun of by a monkey at the zoo, or get chased and sat on by an ostrich?

19. Would you rather brush a hippo's teeth, as a job, or pick cobras for shows from a cage full of cobras?

20. Would you rather get stung by a bunch of electric eels, or get three toes taken off by a hungry alligator?

21. Would you rather take a tyre stuck on the neck of a crocodile off to help it, or help a lion get out a piece of meat stuck in its teeth?

22. Would you rather get swallowed whole by a large blue whale or get stung fatally by a poisonous jellyfish?

23. Would you rather be devoured to the bone by a bunch of piranhas or be slowly digested by a large terrifying snake?

24. Would you rather camp in a site notorious for having violent bears within the vicinity or live on an island full of snakes, each for a month?

25. Would you rather help a squirrel find where it hid its nuts or help a raccoon forage through a waste bin for food?

26. Would you rather get into a food eating contest with a pig, or a swimming and stunts contest with a dolphin?

27. Would you rather walk all the way from work or school with a snail, or have a long understanding heart to heart conversation with a sloth (at their pace)?

28. Would you rather get gored by an elephant's tusks or kicked in the back by a wild horse?

29. Would you rather sleep in a room full of grasshoppers jumping about everywhere, including under the blanket, or eat breakfast in a kitchen full of worms, even in the pots?

30. Would you rather be taken care of by a gorilla in the wild for five years, or live with bush babies in a cage at the zoo for a year, getting bullied by them?

31. Would you rather raise elephants or raise dolphins?

32. Would you rather have a tarantula as a best friend or have a scorpion as an evil friend?

33. Would you rather have quills like a porcupine or fur as soft as a chinchilla?

34. Would you rather hang from trees like a three toed sloth or have sticky feet like a tree frog?

35. Would you rather spend your summer holiday at the beach with many starfish or explore the city with a bunch of rats?

36. Would you rather be raised by a herd of goats or be raised by a herd of cows?

37. Would you rather be an owl or a bat?

38.   Would you rather be a vegetarian forever or catch prey and kill it yourself?

39. Would you rather have a tail like a cat's or a tail as strong as a thresher shark's tail?

40. Would you rather have hoofed feet or have webbed feet?

Animal & Insect Instincts:

What animals' or insects natural defense mechanism would you like to have, and how smart or silly would you choose to be? Let's see as we compare animals' abilities and make animalistic choices!

41. Would you rather be able to attack other sea creatures like a strong but cute Boxer crab or explode like the Malaysian Exploding Ant when you sense danger?

42. Would you rather be able to spray attackers with blood from your eyes like a Texas Horned Lizard or camouflage yourself like a Cuttlefish to avoid attackers?

43. Would you rather be able to excrete toxic cyanide like Cyanide Excreting Millipedes when you sense danger or camouflage as a stick like a stick insect to protect yourself?

44. Would you rather be able to give an electric shock like an electric eel to save yourself or turn to liquid or solid at will like a sea cucumber when trying to escape?

45. Would you rather be able to break your own bones and bring out claws to defend yourself, like a Hairy Frog or break off the tip of your arm to divert attention and escape, like a Deep Sea Squid?

46. Would you rather be able to turn your ribs into spikes like a newt, to defend yourself or bring out slime from your body like a hagfish, to deal with enemies?

47. Would you rather be able to play dead like an Opossum to ward off predators or mimic meerkats like the Drongo bird, to get the meerkats food and survive?

48. Would you rather be able to secrete chemicals from your body like a dart frog, to survive from enemies or squirt foul smelling juice at attackers like a skunk?

49. Would you rather be able to fly or glide away from predators like a flying fish, or vomit smelling stuff like a Turkey Vulture to creep out anyone hunting you down?

50. Would you rather be able to release poison from your armpits like a Slow Loris to defend yourself or run backwards into an attacker with sharp quills, like the African Crested Porcupine?

Cute and Cuddly Factor:

What sort of cute animal would you like to be? Let's find out in this section!

51. Would you rather be a Scottish fold cat or a Persian cat?

52. Would you rather be a Pomeranian Dog or a mini pig?

53. Would you rather be a ferret or a chinchilla?

54. Would you rather be a clown fish or a chameleon?

55. Would you rather be a slow loris or a meerkat?

56. Would you rather be a mini lop rabbit or a Netherland Dwarf rabbit?

57. Would you rather be a sugar glider or an African Pygmy Hedgehog?

58. Would you rather be a baby penguin or a Philippine tarsier?

59. Would you rather be a giant panda or a sloth?

60. Would you rather be a hedgehog or a northern Pygmy Owl?

61. Would you rather be a Koala bear or an Arctic Fox?

62. Would you rather be a Red Panda or a pygmy Hippopotamus?

63. Would you rather be a Fennec Fox or a Tree Kangaroo?

64. Would you rather be a Baiji Dolphin or an American Pika?

65. Would you rather be a bunny or a kinkajou?

66. Would you rather be a Pomeranian Dog or a Black Footed Ferret?

67. Would you rather be a serval or an Axolotl?

68. Would you rather be a Quoll or a Tamandua?

69. Would you rather be a Jerboa or a Maned Wolf?

70. Would you rather be a Black Footed Wild cat or a Bearded Tamarin Monkey?

71. Would you rather be a Wombat or a Clouded Leopard?

72. Would you rather be a Harp Seal or a Field Mouse?

73. Would you rather be a Bongo or a Harris's Antelope Squirrel?

74. Would you rather be a Chevrotain or a Japanese Raccoon Dog?

75. Would you rather be a Gundi or a Siberian Flying Squirrel?

76. Would you rather be an Alpaca or a Harp Seal?

77. Would you rather be a bee hummingbird or a meerkat?

78. Would you rather be a Baluga Whale or a Bottlenose Dolphin?

79. Would you rather be a Sea Otter or an Olinguito?

80. Would you rather be a reindeer or a deer?

Chap 4: Would You Rather: Embarrassing Moments.

Random:

Everyone has moments when they are embarrassed. In such situations where there are only two embarrassing options, its best to go with the one that you can 'live with'. Have fun picking that option that won't get you laughed at - too much.

1. Would you rather go out with totally wet clothes or with lots of mud in your hair?

2. Would you rather wake up and discover you peed on your bed, or wake up to discover that you were sleepwalking and you ate everything in the fridge over the night?

3. Would you rather wear high heels and fall down in front of a crowd, or find out you defecated in your pants, right in front of a crowd?

4. Would you rather have to deal with stage fright that causes everyone to laugh at you, or a really bad temper that has everyone really scared of you?

5. Would you rather dress like someone of the opposite sex for one whole day in public and risk all your friends seeing you or

dress up in a costume as a big duck wearing panties where everyone can see you?

6. Would you rather get caught digging into the celebrant's cake at a party or get caught sleeping during a sermon at church?

7. Would you rather have bullies give you wedgies in front of your crush, or get booed at a talent show on TV?

8. Would you rather get caught drinking the milk out of a babies bottle or get caught/found sleeping in the crib with diapers on?

9. Would you rather get arrested for shoplifting, or caught giving food to animals at the zoo, against the rules?

10. Would you rather get chased around the neighborhood by a clown and get laughed at or get pranked by a couple of kids and get labelled a stupid?

11. Would you rather dress up in clothes with all the colours and your hair dyed all shades strutting round town or dress up as a demon and go round telling people its Halloween when everyone knows its not?

12. Would you rather go round town begging with torn clothes or check bins for food and take whatever people leave at the tables in a restaurant?

13. Would you rather get caught sleeping in class or reading a book that you hid within another book?

14. Would you rather get jailed for driving too fast or drive slowly and get laughed at by an old lady who says you drive like HER grandma?

15. Would you rather go out all day then discover that the back of your pants had been torn all along or raise your hands up forgetting that you haven't shaved and you're as hairy as a forest, in front of a group of friends you're just getting to know for the first time?

16. Would you rather eat to your satisfaction in a fancy restaurant and then discover that you can't pay because you left your wallet at home, so you have to wash dishes, or get your hair and nails done at a saloon and then discover that you can't pay and get your hair cut off?

17. Would you rather have a bunch of dogs chase you up a tree or one dog rips off a piece of your pants ?

18. Would you rather not take a bath for a few days and have everyone running away or pick your nose constantly in front of everyone ?

19. Would you rather break a whole tea set in front of a group of guests or dance on a table like a ballet dancer right in front of them?

20. Would you rather sit next to a guy who eats really messily and then rubs his grubby hands and food all over you, or a lady that totally makes fun of you to her friends all the time when you sit next to her?

21. Would you rather have everyone know that you still pee on the bed or everyone gets to see you totally nude as a baby, in your baby pictures?

22. Would you rather let your crush know that you like really gross food or vomit all over them?

23. Would you rather be caught letting your dog poop in someone else's yard or be caught using another person's bathroom in their house ?

24. Would you rather fail driving lessons hundreds of times or drive your dad's car into the wall and confess that it was you?

25. Would you rather make an embarrassing and unimpressive splash into the pool at a pool party or get into a race at a sports event and totally lose to every other contestant?

26. Would you rather embarrass yourself by dancing in a party where everyone's staring because you can't dance at all, or go to a dance show and totally ruin it in front of the judges?

27. Would you rather be in a situation where you don't know how to use the coffee machine or one where you heap your plate at a buffet and everyone thinks you're a glutton?

28. Would you rather slip over a banana peel in front of a whole class and have them laugh at you, or go round school all day without knowing a note saying 'I'm silly' is on your back the whole time?

29. Would you rather get pinched on the nose by a lobster and you run around the whole restaurant screaming until they get it off, or you would be the cook and burn everyone's food at the restaurant?

30. Would you rather wear a short pink tutu and a wig if you are a boy or baggy jeans, a fake beard and cut your hair if you are a girl? For two days. Or no clothes at all.

31. Would you rather dance weirdly at a club or throw popcorn in the movie theater - at everyone?

32. Would you rather show up for work late with your boss getting angry at you, or come early but have diarrhea, and use the toilet all day?

33. Would you rather get locked out of your car by yourself or get locked out of your house because of your carelessness?

34. Would you rather get stuck on the roof of your house while trying to save your cat, or stuck in a gutter while trying to save your dog?

35. Would you rather cook something that smells terrible or something that tastes terrible?

36. Would you rather have no pens to use in class or no clean clothes to wear at home

37. Would you rather have the wind blow up your skirt or the wind blow off your wig?

38. Would you rather smell like a skunk or smell like poop?

39. Would you rather be caught stealing strawberry ice-cream at home or be caught stealing chocolates from a shop

40. Would you rather ruin someone's new car by mistake or spoil their phone by mistake?

Crush Nightmare:

41. Would you rather let your crush know that you walk around their house for no good reason or that you break in and use their toilet whenever they aren't home?

42. Would you rather scream and run away when your crush asks you on a date or laugh uncontrollably?

43. Would you rather do cartwheels or summersault in front of your crush?

44. Would you rather trip your crush up by mistake or fart in front of your crush?

45. Would you rather punch a crush by mistake or slap a crush by mistake?

46. Would you rather vomit all over your crush or drool on their shoulder while sleeping next to them on the bus home?

47. Would you rather lose to your crush at a video game or win your crush while playing a video game?

48. Would you rather make a joke that your crush doesn't find funny or discuss a subject that bores your crush to tears?

49. Would you rather give the wrong answers to your crush for a classroom or offer to do their homework and totally mess it up?

50. Would you rather destroy your crush's clothes or ruin their shoes by mistake?

51. Would you rather show up with a silly gift for your crush or show up with a pet chicken for your crush?

52. Would you rather crash into a wall while looking at your crush or pour your drink all over yourself while looking at your crush?

53. Would you rather let your crush find pictures of them on your phone or you send your photos to them by mistake?

54. Would you rather let your crush see you with a skin infection or see you with sunburn that makes you look cooked?

55. Would you rather let your crush see you in a really messy wig or see you in oversized clothes?

56. Would you rather get sent out of class in front of your crush or get booed off a stage in front of your crush?

57. Would you rather eat with your hands in front of your crush or get hit with a ball in front of your crush?

58. Would you rather let your crush catch you mimicking them or let your crush catch you gossiping about your friend?

59. Would you rather let your crush see your baby pictures or let your crush see the stuff you liked as a kid?

60. Would you rather buy your crush a book they don't like or clothes they don't like?

Friend Fails:

Those embarrassing moments your friends never fail to forget and laugh about? These are the cringe options you have to pick from...

61. Would you rather send a wrong text to your friend or send a silly picture to your friend by mistake?

62. Would you rather clog the toilet at your friend's house by mistake or accidentally pee on their bed?

63. Would you rather trip and have your friend laugh at you or get chased by a duck and have your friends laugh at you?

64.   Would you rather wave at someone thinking its your friend or tap someone and discover it isn't your friend when they turn around?

65.   Would you rather have your friend walk in on you in the toilet or have your friend catch you farting loudly when you thought you were all alone?

66. Would you rather take your friend out and discover you all can't pay or let your friend see your room in a total mess?

67. Would you rather have a beastie that talks too much or a beastie that laughs too long and too loudly?

68. Would you rather show at a friend's party looking really silly or show up at a friend's house in a duck costume?

69. Would you rather show up at your school wearing a large, ridiculous hat or show up at school with your face painted white?

70. Would you rather go to school with your breath smelling like garlic or go to school with a milk moustache?

71. Would you rather come to school with a big teddy bear or go to school in your pajamas?

72. Would you rather get caught stuffing your mouth with spaghetti or trying to drink many cartons of milk at once?

73. Would you rather lose your voice and talk like a little girl at school or your voice suddenly becomes deep and your body is really small?

74. Would you rather wear your sisters clothes to school or your mom's clothes to school?

75. Would you rather wear flowers in your hair as a boy when going out with your friends or an oversized faded trouser as a lady?

76. Would you rather get bitten by your friends dog or get scratched by your friends cat?

77. Would you rather go round all day with a paper stuck to your back or go round all day with a pen mark where you least expect?

78. Would you rather be scared by your friend in the dark or tickled by your friend in public?

79. Would you rather wear make-up as a boy amongst your friend or wear a fake moustache all day as a girl?

80. Would you rather hit something with your foot and dance around in pain while your friends can see you or bump your head on something that is clearly visible so your friends think you are a clumsy person?

Chap 5: Would You Rather - Beauty and Fashion

Random

Bizarre and annoying situations unfold as one has to pick what silly bodily feature or ridiculous piece of clothing they'd rather be stuck with. Well, it's one unbelievable option or the other.

1. Would you rather have no eyebrows and no hair or a big moustache?

2. Would you rather have long hair growing out of your armpits like Rapunzel, or permanently long finger and toenails that are five feet long?

3. Would you rather have a large mouth that covers almost half your face, or a wide nose that goes from ear to ear?

4. Would you rather have long legs like stilts or be as fat as a room?

5. Would you rather have the tiniest behind ever or the most dirty yellow teeth with very visible holes in them.

6. Would you rather be extremely ugly with wealth and a family, or extremely beautiful with absolutely nothing?

7. Would you rather have large feet that can't fit into shoes, or large hands that can't fit into pockets?

8. Would you rather have large monstrous black zits all over your body or stretch marks that are everywhere, including your face?

9. Would you rather have a partner that's pretty and really dumb or ugly and intelligent, but with a bad attitude?

10. Would you rather have a large hairy unibrow or a beard that's so long that it reaches your feet?

11. Would you rather have a million piercings all over your body, or surgery to make you look like a 'human lizard'?

12. Would you rather have the top of your head flat as a table or very hairy legs, so hairy that the hair poke out when you wear a trouser or a skirt?

13. Would you rather have long nice hair with a totally bald large circle in the middle of your head or a forehead full of pimples?

14. Would you rather have a shapeless body or be almost as thin as a skeleton with almost no flesh on your entire body?

15. Would you rather have an enormous stomach that makes everyone ask if you're pregnant or eyes with large dark patches and bags under the eyes that make you look extremely old?

16. Would you rather have the largest breasts in the world or the largest hips in the world?

17. Would you rather have funny eye lashes that are very very long or natural rings round your neck that are so many, they make you look like a human ostrich?

18. Would you rather have a million freckles that leave very little space left in your face or totally black eyes with no whites in them?

19. Would you rather have itchy irritable skin or skin that is totally blue or green in color?

20. Would you rather have a long tail that you can't hide or an animal's snout as a nose?

21. Would you rather have scales like a fish on your entire body or have to molt out of your skin every three months; you would have to shed off the skin on your body and regrow it for a week?

22. Would you rather have no skin at all with all your veins and internal organs showing, or abnormally thick skin that leaves you hot all the time?

23. Would you rather have bright red cheeks worse than a clown's painted ones, or eyes that shimmer so brightly nobody can look into them, or they'd go blind?

24. Would you rather have long arms that leave your hands almost touching the floor, or an elastic chin that makes you look like a turkey, it flabs and hangs down your entire chest?

25. Would you rather have permanent body odor that you can't get rid of, or extremely sensitive skin that needs extremely expensive care?

26. Would you rather have ears that look like sponges or a nose full of holes?

27. Would you rather have alien features, big black eyes and head and funny skin, or features of a monster like creature that also comes from space?

28. Would you rather have a long neck that makes your head reach the ceiling or a shell on your back, like a tortoise?

29. Would you rather be too tall or extremely short?

30. Would you rather have permanent blush on your cheeks that makes you look embarrassed all the time or permanent lipstick that makes your lips look large and stand out too much all the time?

31. Would you rather be overdressed all the time or be underdressed all the time?

32. Would you rather wear absolutely glitzy clothes and a large ridiculous wig or a very dull outfit that is a bit worn out?
33. Would you rather look like a monkey with make up on or a shark with make up on?

34. Would you rather have spines on your legs or tongues growing everywhere on your face?

35. Would you rather dress in neon green all the time or neon pink all the time?

36. Would you rather wear super high heels all the time or never wear heels for the rest of your life?

37. Would you rather dye your hair in a crazy color or shave almost all your hair off with one spot left in the middle?

38. Would you rather wear a fur coat in the summer or thin clothes during winter?

39. Would you rather always put on lipstick that is too bold or never wear make up for the rest of your life?

40. Would you rather dye your eyebrows green or fix really funny looking nails?

Social Statements:

The last thing you'd get caught wearing outside? Or at an event? Time to face some gruesome choices about what sort of embarrassment you can actually deal with.

41.   Would you rather wear cargo pants forever or wear popped collars forever?

42. Would you rather attend a party with your friends in gym clothes or sleep in really tight uncomfortable clothes?

43. Would you rather wear a funny Halloween costume or a sexy Halloween costume?

44. Would you rather wear matching shirts with a pet or matching shirts with your best friend?

45. Would you rather have the same pendant as your cat or same pendant as your dog?

46. Would you rather wear only 70's clothing or sport an 80's haircut?

47. Would you rather have a closet with only brightly colored clothes or a closet with only black clothes?

48. Would you rather get ten new piercings or a tattoo on your face?

49. Would you rather wear the same clothes as your enemy or beautiful dresses and clothes that everyone has?

50. Would you rather always have a bad hair day or dirty clothes?

Fashion Fails or Fashion Finesse?

Sometimes it's all glam and sometimes we make fashion mistakes and feel like a clam. So, what if we get stuck with a particular flaw or finesse forever? Check out the following, which options would you be able to live with...or without?

51. Would you rather wear ugly yoga pants every day or funny looking jeans every day?

52. Would you rather wear only trucker hats with all outfits or bucket hats with all outfits?

53. Would you rather wear socks with sandals on a first date or ugly shoes on a first date?

54. Would you rather wear only face caps with every outfit for life or wear a fez on every outfit for life?

55. Would you rather wear a stained shirt to a high class event or something covered in cat hair?

56. Would you rather dress like an 80's girl forever or dress like you're eighty forever?

57. Would you rather wear white clothes always or black clothes always?

58. Would you rather wear non - prescription glasses as a fashion statement or sunglasses at night as a fashion statement?

59. Would you rather wear outfits straight out of the 1920's or outfits straight out of the 1970's?

60. Would you rather wear clothes like a hippie forever or clothes like a goth forever?

61. Would you rather wear things made out of cotton or things made out of linen?

62. Would you rather wear clothes with cartoon prints or those with no prints at all?

63. Would you rather wear totally worn out clothes or dirty clothes?

64. Would you rather wear all pink clothes or all blue?

65. Would you rather wear ugly expensive clothes or cheap, beautiful clothes made with low quality fabrics?

66. Would you rather wear a tutu to a business conference or a suit to a t-shirt family party?

67. Would you rather wear a top hat or a fez cap?

68. Would you rather wear a pleated skirt or a long skirt?

69. Would you rather wear a grey wig or a white wig?

70. Would you rather use perfume that smells like flowers or perfumes that smell like food?

71. Would you rather wear a crown made of diamonds or a crown made of gold?

72. Would you rather wear head bands and wrist bands all the time or earrings and piercings all the time?

73. Would you rather wear tight clothing for a day or clothing that is oversized for a day?

74. Would you rather dress up with a bit of glitter every day or wear fashionable glasses every day?

75. Would you rather wear pearls or silver necklaces?

76. Would you rather wear your hair in a bun all the time or let your hair down all the time?

77. Would you rather wear turtlenecks forever or half tops forever?

78. Would you rather wear silver socks or lace socks?

79. Would you rather wear frilly gowns or glittery gowns?

80. Would you rather wear red clothes that make you look like a stoplight or green clothes that make you look like a walking plant?

Chap 6: Would You Rather - Food

Random:

Anything and everything about food, the desirable and the disgusting. Let's see how many choices will be made...

1. Would you rather eat soup that is full of hot pepper with no water close by, or drink a whole bottle of ketchup?

2. Would you rather try an exotic meal which might kill you, or eat sea animals that are half alive and totally weird to you?

3. Would you rather eat baby rats dipped in sauce or drink a bottle of snake wine - with the snake still in the bottle?

4. Would you rather eat a worm sandwich or centipedes and spaghetti?

5. Would you rather have a dish with some of the cooks nails in the food, or some soup that has nothing wrong with it but a dead fly floating on top of it?

6. Would you rather eat a meal of roasted insects or frozen edible leaves with living ants all over them?

7. Would you rather a special delicacy of rotten cheese that stinks and has worms coming out of it, on a piece of bread, or eat edible soil?

8. Would you rather drink ten bottles of water mixed with cow pee or one bottle of slug juice with a little bit of salt mixed in?

9. Would you rather eat a dead seagull raw or a roasted pigeon cooked with pigeon eggs too?

10. Would you rather eat frog legs nicely prepared with some sauce or a delicious meal made out of pig's blood?

11. Would you rather eat poisonous mushrooms or a prickly cactus?

12. Would you rather drink milk and chicken skin blended together, or eat a pizza covered with vegetables?

13. Would you rather eat a meat pie with cooked bugs in it, or fish pie made with piranhas, complete down to their sharp teeth and scales?

14. Would you rather eat a lot of cat food or a lot of doggie treats?

15. Would you rather slurp up twenty raw eggs at once or a lot of Aloe Vera gel?

16. Would you rather have a meal of stew made with a thousand fish eyes or stew made with plenty of fish eggs?

17. Would you rather eat cats, cooked as a meal, which some people do eat or some well prepared dog meat?

18. Would you rather eat a baby's thrown up meal or a snake dish that you have to eat carefully because the snake might still be alive and could still bite you?

19. Would you rather eat some turtles eggs, or have some pieces of a large boiled ostrich egg?

20. Would you rather eat a pizza with nothing on it, or some tasteless food with no spices at all?

21. Would you rather cook a balding, sick vulture or a really dirty dying platypus for dinner?

22. Would you rather eat a pie with some poisoned berries in it or eat a few poisonous mushrooms?

23. Would you rather have mud and slime mixed with chocolate, or coconut candy with skunk hairs in it?

24. Would you rather eat fried chicken's feet or fried alligators feet?

25. Would you rather have fries and sheep's brain or a pie filled with animals cooked guts, intestines?

26. Would you rather eat tadpoles alive or a living goldfish?

27. Would you rather eat vegetables only for a week or just mangoes and water, the entire week?

28. Would you rather eat a meal made of a ram's head or rice mixed with rat tails?

29. Would you rather eat fifteen spicy noodles with only a bottle of water, or about thirty sweet treats with absolutely no water to drink afterwards?

30. Would you rather have a meal of anteaters snout and sauce, or ten locust sandwiches?

31. Would you rather eat a small can of cat food, or a bunch of rotten cucumbers?

32. Would you rather eat a spoonful of wasabi or a cup of soy sauce?

33. Would you rather eat a plate of uncooked meat or drink a cup of spoiled milk?

34. Would you rather never eat butter/cheese again or never eat spaghetti again?

35. Would you rather eat a whole lemon or drink a cup of olive oil?

36. Would you rather have no sweets for the rest of your life or no spicy foods for the rest of your life?

37. Would you rather eat 200 marshmallows in one sitting or have twenty scoops of ice cream in one sitting?

38. Would you rather drink a whole large bottle of tomato juice or drink a bottle of lemon juice every day of the week?

39. Would you rather eat fifteen boiled eggs or twenty pieces of fried meat?

40. Would you rather eat chocolate forever or eat ice cream forever?

Crazy Combinations:

Do you think you've seen it all? Here are some of the weirdest food combinations ever to pick from.

41. Would you rather have cold pizza dipped in soda or ketchup and pizza?

42. Would you rather eat popcorn and hot sauce or popcorn and black pepper?

43. Would you rather take hot chocolate with cheese or cheddar cheese with apple pie?

44. Would you rather snack on a peanut butter and pickle sandwich or peanut butter and goat cheese?

45. Would you rather eat pepper and a chocolate ice cream or a coca cola drink mixed with ketchup?

46. Would you rather eat ice cream and olive oil or a burger mixed with peanut butter?

47. Would you rather eat boursin cheese and doritos or grilled pineapple with tabasco sauce?

48. Would you rather eat strawberries and balsamic vinegar or Greek yogurt and black pepper?

49. Would you rather eat crackers and peanut butter or salami and grapes?

50. Would you rather eat mayonnaise and grape jelly sandwich or apple juice and goldfish biscuits?

Let's Get Exotic!

In this part of the *Would You Rather* Food Section, strange edibles and non - edible's from countries all around the world are provided for your taste! Pick an option if you dare, and then check at the bottom of the section to see if you picked something 'to eat, or NOT to eat'. Anyone who 'survives' by picking an edible meal, gets five points. 'Poisonous picks' where the player has chosen an inedible food will mean the player gets no points. Can you take the risk? Let's see!

51. Would you rather have bittersweet berries or tomatillo?

52. Would you rather eat soap nuts or borscht?

53. Would you rather have a few slices of sea cucumber or three potato fruits?

54. Would you rather eat a poison dart frog or a sea urchin?

55. Would you rather eat a blue ringed octopus or a geoduck?

56. Would you rather have squid ink ice cream or tansy tea?

57. Would you rather eat rhubarb leaves or cassia bark?

58. Would you rather eat radiatori pasta or raw dough?

59. Would you rather eat a lotus flower or a daffodil?

60. Would you rather eat a plate of seasoned fish eyes or bitter almonds?

61. Would you rather have some cone snail delicacy or fried starfish?

62. Would you rather have bird's nest soup or snowberries?

63. Would you rather drink snake wine or eat a blowfish?

64. Would you rather eat a giant hogweed or romanesco?

65. Would you rather have some dandelion jelly or raw kidney beans?

66. Would you rather have some buttercup salad or kumquat?

67. Would you rather eat a dish made of okra soup and yam flour or some lovely fabergé eggs?

68. Would you rather eat knedlik or rafflesia?

69. Would you rather indulge in some durian fruit or a tube of toothpaste?

70. Would you rather cook an armadillo or eat three century eggs?

71. Would you rather eat baby octopus tentacles or drink some sea water?

72. Would you rather eat gooseneck barnacles or some strips of rotten shark meat?

73. Would you rather eat a prickly pear or some coral?

74. Would you rather eat fried bull's testicles or toadstool?

75. Would you rather eat a 'crunchy' rooster's comb or have some grilled shell fungi?

76. Would you rather eat lipstick or water leaf soup?

77. Would you rather eat escargot or mandrake?

78. Would you rather eat mistletoe or kalakukko?

79. Would you rather eat skunk meat or chicken feet?

80. Would you rather eat hawksbill turtle or fried snake meat?

	EDIBLE	NON - EDIBLE
51.	Tomatillo	Bittersweet Berries
52.	Borscht	Soap nuts
53.	Sea cucumber	Potato fruit
54.	Sea urchin	Poison dart frog.
55.	Geoduck	Blue ringed octopus
56.	Squid ink ice cream	Tansy tea
57.	Cassia Bark	Rhubarb leaves
58.	Radiatori Pasta	Raw Dough
59.	Lotus Flower	Daffodil
60.	Fish Eyes	Bitter Almonds
61.	Fried Starfish	Cone snail
62.	Bird's nest soup	Snowberries
63.	Snake Wine	Blowfish
64.	Giant Hogweed	Romanesco
65.	Dandelion jelly	Raw kidney beans
66.	Kumquat	Buttercup Salad
67.	Okra Soup and Yam Flour	Fabergé Eggs
68.	Knedlik	Rafflesia
69.	Durian Fruit	Toothpaste

70.	Armadillo	Century Eggs
71.	Baby Octopus Tentacles	Sea water
72.	Gooseneck barnacles	Rotten Shark
73.	Prickly Pear	Coral
74.	Fried Bull's Testicles	Toadstool
75.	Rooster's Comb	Grilled Shell Fungi
76.	Water Leaf Soup	Lipstick
77.	Escargot	Mandrake
78.	Kalakukko	Mistletoe
79.	Chicken Feet	Skunk meat
80.	Hawksbill Turtle	Snake Meat

Chap 7: Would You Rather - Love and Friendship

Random:

Love is all that matters, right? Let love fill the air as you make some rose scented choices. Some choices may be a bit embarrassing, but at the end of the day, love is unconditional. Love your choices!

1. Would you rather fall in love with someone 'at first sight' or fall in love gradually?

2. Would you rather watch the sun set with your loved ones or watch the sunrise with your loved ones?

3. Would you rather have a girlfriend or boyfriend that argues all the time or one that never gives you a kiss?

4. Would you rather sing in your car with your family or sing karaoke with your family?

5. Would you rather be single or be in a relationship?

6. Would you rather eat a meal with your crush without cutlery or sing them a love song with a milk moustache?

7. Would you rather have a friend tell you they love you or tell your friend that you love him/her?

8. Would you rather go out for ice cream with your family or have sundaes at home with your family?

9. Would you rather have a crush that is really funny or have a crush that is super intelligent?

10. Would you rather have a soulmate or a million dollars?

11. Would you rather be friends with someone that loves your friends or be friends with someone that loves your family?

12. Would you rather hear 'I love you' every ten seconds or hear 'I love you' only once in a year?

13. Would you rather be friends with someone that your family loves or be friends with someone that your friends love?

14. Would you rather let your crush see you with spaghetti all over your shirt or let your crush see you with tuna rubbed all over your face?

15. Would you rather have a friend slam a cake into your face or have a friend pour a fizzy drink into your hair?

16. Would you rather exchange shoes with your best friend or exchange hats with your best friend?

17. Would you rather be your own best friend for a day, or go on a picnic with all your friends?

18. Would you rather swap phones with your boyfriend or girlfriend or swap rooms with your boyfriend or girlfriend?

19. Would you rather gulp down a drink loudly in front of your crush or slurp spaghetti loudly in front of your crush?

20. Would you rather climb a few mountains with your family or swim across a few lakes with your family?

21. Would you rather have your family members exchange nice notes with each other or you would prefer to put nice notes under everyone's pillows?

22. Would you rather give your friends a candy treat or take your family on a surprise outing?

23. Would you rather buy a strong and sweet perfume for your beloved or get them ten boxes of chocolate?

24. Would you rather have a band sing for your beloved or have their names written in clouds?

25. Would you rather stay indoors or go out on a date?

26. Would you rather watch a comedy movie with your family or watch a horror movie with your family?

27. Would you rather go to a fancy restaurant with your beloved or eat at home with your beloved?

28. Would you rather let your crush see you in a clown suit or let your crush see that you pooped in your pants?

29. Would you rather share lunch with your loved ones or share dinner with your celebrity crush?

30. Would you rather buy a house on the beach for your loved ones or buy a house in the city for your loved ones?

Crush Country:

We all have the one, two or three people that we really like and are literally obsessed with. What's that situation you would prefer to be in with your crush? Choose that - over a worse fate. Try to decide without blushing so much your face goes completely red.

31. Would you rather get a kiss on the cheek from your crush after a first date or a kiss on the forehead?

32. Would you rather get hugs from your crush or lots of compliments?

33. Would you rather say something nice to your crush to make them blush or say something funny to make them laugh?

34. Would you rather give your crush a card or give them flowers?

35. Would you rather go out to watch a movie with your crush or stay indoors with your crush to watch a movie?

36. Would you rather have your crush get jealous or have them get angry at you?

37. Would you rather hold hands with your crush or get a peck from your crush?

38. Would you rather write a love letter to your crush or get a love letter from them?

39. Would you rather go on an outing with a high school crush or a night out with a celebrity crush?

40. Would you rather blow a kiss to your crush or wink at your crush?

41. Would you rather sing to your crush in public or sing to your crush in private?

42. Would you rather shower your crush with gifts or shower your crush with money?

43. Would you rather go on a surprise road trip with your crush or go on a surprise vacation with your crush?

44. Would you rather wear your crush's shirt or wear your crush's skirt/trouser?

45. Would you rather have your crush go after you or you would go after your crush?

46. Would you rather take photos at a photo booth with your crush or take silly selfies with them at home?

47. Would you rather chase your crush round a beach or chase your crush round a park?

48. Would you rather draw pictures in the sand with your crush or draw hearts in the sand with your crush?

49. Would you rather throw water balloons at your crush or spray water on your crush with a hose?

50. Would you rather dance under moonlight with your crush or dance under the rain with your crush?

Celebrity:

Talking about crushes, what celebrities or social giants do you have a mad obsession with? Who would you rather meet?

51. Would you rather have tea with Margot Robbie or go out for ice cream with Ed Sheeran?

52. Would you rather go on a boat ride with Adam Driver or drive Dr Phil McGraw to work?

53. Would you rather hug Beyoncé or give Rihanna a peck on the cheek?

54. Would you rather blow a kiss to Kevin Hart or draw a picture for Donald Glover?

55. Would you rather sing for Ellen DeGeneres or rap for Jay Z?

56. Would you rather write a book for J.K. Rowling or dedicate a song to Elton John?

57. Would you rather have lunch with Ryan Seacrest or go on a picnic with Adele?

58. Would you rather do a silly dance to make Chris Hemsworth laugh or make jokes to get Taylor Swift to laugh?

59. Would you rather do a show with Justin Bieber or go to a party with Sean Combs?

60. Would you rather watch a movie with Jackie Chan or watch a movie at home with Anthony Joshua?

61. Would you rather perform on stage with Pink or dance with Katy Perry?

62. Would you rather go on a date with Dwayne Johnson or go on a date with Justin Timberlake?

63. Would you rather pull pranks on people with Bruno Mars or pull a prank on Chris Pratt?

64. Would you rather make faces at Miley Cyrus or do a strange chicken dance in front of Kylie Jenna?

65. Would you rather kiss DJ Khalid on the cheek or give Steve Harvey a hug?

66. Would you rather live with The Chainsmokers or travel with Celine Dion?

67. Would you rather share lunch with Drake or dinner with Chris Pratt?

68. Would you rather act in a movie with Jennifer Lawrence or sing karaoke with Ariana Grande?

69. Would you rather play football with Lionel Messi or play football with Christiano Ronaldo?

70. Would you rather rap with Eminem or go on a road trip with Billy Joel?

71. Would you rather live with Leonardo DiCaprio or live with Emily Blunt?

72. Would you rather be featured in Kanye West's video or be featured in Donald Glover's video?

73. Would you rather run after Rita Ora or Demi Lovato?

74. Would you rather bake a cake for Lady Gaga or Shawn Mendes?

75. Would you rather give Shakira a massage or wash Madonna's hair?

76. Would you rather go on a date with Camilla Cabello or picnic with Zayn Malik?

77. Would you rather sing with Billie Eilish or Sam Smith?

78. Would you rather take a walk with Chris Brown or Nick Jonas?

79. Would you rather invite Lady Gaga to your birthday party or Kevin Hart?

80. Would you rather go to a party with J. Cole or J.K Rowling?

Chap 8: Would You Rather - Technology.

Random:

What do you like about tech and what don't you like? Let's go!

1. Would you rather have free WiFi or three new phones?

2. Would you rather get all the apps you want for free or all the games you want for free?

3. Would you rather have a laptop that's fairly used or a phone that's really old?

4. Would you rather own an old TV or a radio?

5. Would you rather lose your password or lose all your apps?

6. Would you rather have a car that drives itself or a car that can transform into a robot?

7. Would you rather have spy glasses or a pen with a camera?

8.   Would you rather have a car with guns attached or a car that can camouflage?

9. Would you rather own a smart watch or an iPad?

10. Would you rather own Twitter or Instagram?

11. Would you rather own Facebook or WhatsApp?

12. Would you rather give up your home theater or your PlayStation?

13. Would you rather burn all your books or by a Kindle ready?

14.   Would you rather have a lifelong subscription of iTunes or a lifelong subscription of App store?

15. Would you rather never laugh again or never use your cellphone again?

16. Would you rather use a Mac or a PC?

17. Would you rather use a smartphone or a blackberry?

18. Would you rather work for Google or Facebook?

19. Would you rather play computer games or just sleep?

20. Would you rather use your computer or watch TV?

21. Would you rather pick color or monochrome?

22. Would you rather like the red Pokémon game or the blue Pokémon game?

23. Would you rather play Supermario land or Tetris?

24. Would you rather use VHS cassettes or Records?

25. Would you rather use the apple operating system or Microsoft word operating system?'

26. Would you rather use android or is?

27. Would you rather have a Bugatti or a Camero?

28. Would you rather use Intel or amd?

29. Would you rather have your computer stolen or your tablet stolen?

30. Would you rather use linux or windows?

Social Media Situation:

Our phones are literally our babies these days. There are things that could drive us beserk if they ever happened, especially when it comes to our various accounts on social media. From all sort of hacks to invasion of privacy, we have to pick a particular internet nightmare!

31. Would you rather be stalker on social media or disturbed by many trolls?

32. Would you rather be attacked by a group of trolls or snooped on by one very creepy person?

33. Would you rather be accosted on social media with an open letter or favorite the wrong tweet?

34. Would you rather be retweeted after posting your worst tweet or post a tweet with a typo?

35. Would you rather accidentally like a random photo or accidentally like your crushes photo ?

36. Would you rather tag the wrong person or tag a whole bunch of friends on an embarrassing photo?

37. Would you rather be shocked that your parents are your friends on social media or get annoying comments from family members on a photo?

38. Would you rather be thrilled with new followers but they are bots or have new followers and they are annoying?

39. Would you rather accidentally follow someone on social media or get zero likes on social media?

40. Would you rather have your account taken down or have your account hacked?

41. Would you rather date someone from social media or enter a challenge on social media?

42. Would you rather be known on twitter or known on Instagram?

43. Would you rather be known on Facebook or known on WhatsApp?

44. Would you rather have Snapchat or Likee?

45. Would you rather be a social media influencer or a blogger?

46. Would you rather be a troll or an annoying Youtuber?

47. Would you rather be a celebrity on Instagram or a celebrity on Facebook?

48. Would you rather accidentally like your most annoying friend's post on facebook or allow them to chat you up on WhatsApp?

49. Would you rather be caught stalking someone on social media or catch someone stalking you?

50. Would you rather swap phones with your best friend or swap phones with your crush?

51. Would you rather show your parents your search history or show your siblings your search history?

52. Would you rather have internet access all the time and no laptop or laptop but no internet?

53. Would you rather have slow and free internet or fast but paid for internet services?

54. Would you rather eat the same food forever or never use Instagram again?

55. Would you rather eat ice cream forever or have social media forever?

56. Would you rather lose your keys or forget your cell phone?

57. Would you rather be lonely and have a phone or have friends around you but no phone?

58. Would you rather be stung by a jellyfish and have Facebook or not get stung and have no Facebook?

59. Would you rather get prevent from shopping or give up emoji?

60. Would you rather watch TV all the time or not at all?

61. Would you rather be chased by a bear and have your tech gadgets or not be chased and have no tech gadgets, no phone, etc?

62. Would you rather be kissed by a roach and stay on Twitter, or not get kissed by a roach and lose your account?

63. Would you rather not upload pictures for five years or not use a phone for five years?

64. Would you rather cut your fingers to get to your phone or cut your toes to reach your laptop?

65. Would you rather be called weird and have your social media accounts or be normal and have no access to social media?

66. Would you rather be lost in the forest but with free WIFI or lost in the city with no internet connection at all?

67. Would you rather have siblings but no tech for the rest of your life or not have siblings but have all the phones and advanced technology?

68. Would you rather live without a cellphone or news?

69. Would you rather play you in Supermario or Minecraft?

70. Would you rather have free internet for life or free food for life

71. Would you rather have infinite battery life for your phone or constant fuel for your car?

72. Would you rather surf the internet or shop until you drop?

73. Would you rather never eat chocolate or have ten phones?

74. Would you rather have no new clothes or have no internet service?

75. Would you rather have the end of face to face conversations or the end of internet connections?

76. Would you rather buy a Canon or a Nikon?

77. Would you rather have Facebook or an iPhone?

78. Would you rather play Mortal Kombat 9 or Call of Duty?

79. Would you rather have Safari or Firefox?

80. Would you rather have a Galaxy S111 or iPhone 4s?

Chap 9: Would You Rather - Luxury & Riches/Travel & Leisure

Random:

Super Rich or super adventurous? Cruise through this section and relax as you make great choices!

1. Would you rather own your private jet or your own train?

2. Would you rather have a closet that is like a clothes shop or lots of shoes that have a whole room to themselves?

3. Would you rather have a personal assistant or a butler?

4. Would you rather have your own restaurant or your own personal chef?

5. Would you rather have ten large mansions or twenty expensive cars?

6. Would you rather get a million dollars cake or a million dollars refreshment for everyone?

7. Would you rather watch TV all day or listen to music all day?

8. Would you rather go to a sleepover or a birthday party

9. Would you rather go and camp in the wild or live in a rural village?

10. Would you rather go to a music festival or hang out at the beach?

11. Would you rather watch a movie with your family at the house or watch a movie at the theater?

12. Would you rather have the most expensive dress in the world or the most expensive chain?

13. Would you rather listen to a violin being played or a guitar getting plays?

14. Would you rather only listen to rock music or listen to country music?

15. Would you rather have a diamond studded phone or a diamond studded laptop?

16. Would you rather have the most expensive pet in the world or the most expensive jewelry?

17. Would you rather own islands or own forests?

18. Would you rather own a music record label or a movie company?

19. Would you rather eat at a restaurant alone, or go and watch a movie with friends?

20. Would you rather be waited on by servants all day or have one professional personal assistant that costs more to maintain?

21. Would you rather own large flower fields or large rose gardens?

22. Would you rather attend all the religious gatherings in the world or all the social events in the world.

23. Would you rather go on a road trip with the family or travel round the world alone?

24. Would you rather have the most expensive foods or the most expensive drinks in the world?

25. Would you rather own a few houses in the area or an amusement park?

26. Would you rather give all your money to charity or take orphans out every week?

27. Would you rather have an expensive hairdo or an expensive manicure and pedicure?

28. Would you rather be worth 40billion dollars or have every member of your family including you be worth 10 billion dollars each?

29. Would you rather get all the celebrities to sing at your birthday party or get them all to attend a party with you?

30. Would you rather eat out of diamond plates or eat out of silver ones.

Exciting Events:

What events would you like to attend around the world. Take a pick from two exciting options!

31. Would you rather go to the Italy Grand Prix, Monza, Italy, or Le Tour De France?

32. Would you rather go to The Masters, Augusta, GA, or The US Open, New York?

33. Would you rather go to FIFA world cup or UEFA Champions League?

34. Would you rather go to the Camden Windjammer Festival, Camden, or the Carnival, Rio Dee Janeiro?

35. Would you rather go to Chinese New Year, Shanghai, China, or Mardi Gras Festival, New Orleans, LA?

36. Would you rather go to the Sapporo Snow Festival or St. Patrick's Day, Dublin, Ireland?

37. Would you rather go Austin, TX, for the Austin City Limits or Coachella Music Festival, Indio.

38. Would you rather go to Sasquatch Music Festival or the Rubber Duck Race, Germany?

39. Would you rather go to the Dragon Boat Carnival, Hong Kong, or Royal Ascot Races, Berkshire, UK?

40. Would you rather go to the World Bog Snorkelling Championships, Wales, or The Winter Games?

41. Would you rather go to The Summer Games or the Cricket World Cup?

42. Would you rather go to Wimbledon, London, UK or Alpine World Ski Championships?

43. Would you rather go to the Rugby World Cup or Daytona 500, Daytona Beach?

44.   Would you rather go to Oktoberfest, Munich, Germany, or the Running of the Bulls, Pamplona, Spain?

45.   Would you rather go to the Carnival of Venice or Elephant Festival, India?

46.   Would you rather go to the Snow and Ice Festival, China, or Tomorrowland, Belgium?

47.   Would you rather go to New Orleans Jazz and Heritage Festival or Wexford Opera Festival, Ireland?

48.   Would you rather go to Venice Biennale, Italy or the Cannes Film Festival , Cannes?

49.   Would you rather go to the Sundance Film Festival, Park City, or Art Deco Weekend, Miami?

50.   Would you rather go to the Day of the Dead, Mexico City, Mexico or La Tomatina, Valencia, Spain?

Travel Train:

What places have you dreamed of traveling to? What places have you dreamed of NEVER traveling to? The family can know your preferences, at least then everyone can know why someone is making a fuss when next they need to travel!

51. Would you rather travel to Albania or Portugal?

52. Would you rather travel to Bolivia or the Philippines?

53. Would you rather travel to Turkey or Mexico?

54. Would you rather travel to Wales or Slovenia?

55. Would you rather travel to Austria or the Netherlands?

56. Would you rather travel to Nepal or Croatia?

57. Would you rather travel to South Africa or Sri Lanka?

58. Would you rather travel to Kenya or Greece?

59. Would you rather travel to Vietnam or Thailand?

60. Would you rather travel to Spain or India?

61. Would you rather travel to Colombia or New Zealand?

62. Would you rather travel to Australia or Switzerland?

63. Would you rather travel to Morocco or USA?

64. Would you rather travel to Canada or Iceland?

65. Would you rather travel to Japan or France?

66. Would you rather travel to Taiwan or Ireland?

67. Would you rather travel to America or Italy?

68. Would you rather travel to Honduras or Belize?

69. Would you rather travel to Burundi and Zambia?

70. Would you rather travel to Haiti or Chile?

71. Would you rather travel to Burkina Faso or Singapore?

72. Would you rather travel to Pakistan or Costa Rica?

73. Would you rather travel to Nigeria or China?

74. Would you rather travel to Lebanon or Nicaragua?

75. Would you rather travel to Peru or Egypt?

76. Would you rather travel to Iran or Saudi Arabia?

77. Would you rather travel to Brazil or Ghana?

78. Would you rather travel to Somalia or Jamaica?

79. Would you rather travel to Guyana or Syria?

80. Would you rather travel to Bangladesh or North Korea?

Bonus game: take the globe and find out all together where all this countries are hidden. How many of those countries you have already visited? Where you will like to travel on your next vacation?

Chap 10: Would You Rather - Sports and Exercises.

Random:

Sports and exercises need a lot of strength, endurance and perseverance. What sports would you rather participate in and how much could you possibly endure? It's the 'Would You Rather' Olympics...and we will see who gets the gold medal!

1. Would you rather participate in Golf or Badminton?

2. Would you rather participate in Football or Baseball?

3. Would you rather participate in Volleyball or Kabaddi?

4. Would you rather participate in Motorcycle Racing or Fencing?

5. Would you rather participate in Polo or Archery?

6. Would you rather participate in Canadian Football or Weightlifting?

7. Would you rather participate in Shooting or Bowling?

8. Would you rather participate in Darts or Sailing?

9. Would you rather participate in Cycling or Swimming?

10. Would you rather participate in Diving or Boxing?

11. Would you rather participate in Wrestling or Cricket?

12. Would you rather participate in Autoracing or Tennis?

13. Would you rather participate in Basketball or Soccer?
14. Would you rather spend the day surfing or running races?

15. Would you rather participate in Dog Surfing or Lawnmower Racing?

16. Would you rather participate in Gurney Contests or Man vs Horse Marathon?

17. Would you rather participate in Redneck Games or Wheelbarrow Racing?

18. Would you rather participate in Wife carrying or unicycle Hockey?

19. Would you rather skydive or go canoeing?

20. Would you rather participate in Chess Boxing or Pato?

21. Would you rather participate in Sepak Takraw or Roller Derby?

22. Would you rather participate in Quidditch or Tuna Tossing?

23. Would you rather participate in Toe wrestling or Arm Wrestling?

24. Would you rather participate in Hotdog Eating Contests or Caber Tossing?

25. Would you rather go bicycling in the mountains or go bungee jumping?

26. Would you rather participate in Bog Snorkelling or Extreme Ironing?

27. Would you rather participate in Cheese Rolling or Giant Pumpkin Kayaking?

28. Would you rather participate in Underwater Football or Competitive Worm Charming?

29. Would you rather participate in Log Rolling or Bubble Soccer?

30. Would you rather participate in Cycleball or Pumpkin Chucking?

Energetic Exercises:

What exercises would you rather commit to or never ever do? Here's a list of the laziest and most strenuous exercises for the team!

31. Would you rather do thirty minutes of kettlebell swings or one hour of pull ups?

32. Would you rather exercise by running three miles every day, or walking up twenty flights on stairs every day?

33. Would you rather do thirty minutes of jogging or one hour of cycling on hills?

34. Would you rather do thirty minutes of softball or one hour of basketball?

35.   Would you rather do thirty minutes of brisk walking or one hour of racquetball?

36. Would you rather do thirty minutes of cycling on level streets or one hour of aerobic dancing?

37.   Would you rather do thirty minutes of running or one hour of calisthenics?

38. Would you rather do thirty minutes of swimming laps or one hour of aerobics?

39. Would you rather do thirty minutes of jumping rope or one hour of yoga?

40. Would you rather do thirty minutes of hiking uphill or one hour of aerobic dancing?

41. Would you rather do thirty minutes of Planks or one hour of Calf Raises?

42. Would you rather do thirty minutes of or one hour of

43. Would you rather do thirty minutes of Bavarian Split Squats or one hour of Dead Lifts?

44. Would you rather do thirty minutes of Bridges or one hour of High Knees?

45. Would you rather do thirty minutes of pushups or one hour of Lunges?

46. Would you rather do thirty minutes of Jumping Jacks or one hour of Squad Jumps?

47. Would you rather do thirty minutes of deep squats or one hour of crunches?

48. Would you rather do thirty minutes of upright barbell row or one hour of sit ups?

49. Would you rather do thirty minutes of Chest flyes on a stability Ball or one hour of free weight front squats?

50. Would you rather do thirty minutes of box jumps or one hour of cable chops?

Sweetest Sports :

Those ones you'll spend all day doing and never seem to get tired of? The sports you can't stand for even a minute? We'll get to your favorites hopefully. This is just a 'warm up' routine.

51. Would you rather have an hour of Giant Pumpkin Kayaking or a day of toe wrestling?

52. Would you rather have an hour of Tuna tossing or a day of Quidditch?

53. Would you rather have an hour of Unicycle Hockey or a day of Chess Boxing?

54. Would you rather have an hour of weightlifting or a day of Archery?

55. Would you rather have an hour of shooting or a day of Bowling?

56. Would you rather have an hour of darts or a day of Dog surfing?

57. Would you rather have an hour of Lawnmower racing or a day of Gurney Contests?

58. Would you rather have an hour of sailing or a day of Man vs Horse Marathon?

59. Would you rather have an hour of Redneck Games or a day of Wheelbarrow Racing?

60. Would you rather have an hour of Wife carrying or a day of Bog Snorkelling?

61. Would you rather have an hour of Extreme Ironing or a day of Cheese Rolling?

62. Would you rather have an hour of Underwear Football or a day of Bubble Soccer?

63. Would you rather have an hour of Cycleball or a day of Competitive Worm Charming?

64. Would you rather have an hour of Log Rolling or a day of Pumpkin Chucking?

65. Would you rather have an hour of Golf or a day of Badminton?

66. Would you rather have an hour of football or a day of Baseball?

67. Would you rather have an hour of Volleyball or a day of Kabaddi ?

68. Would you rather have an hour of Motorcycle Racing or a day of Fencing?

69. Would you rather have an hour of Polo or a day of cycling?

70. Would you rather have an hour of swimming or a day of boxing?

71. Would you rather have an hour of Wrestling or a day of Cricket?

72. Would you rather have an hour of Autoracing or a day of Tennis?

73. Would you rather have an hour of Basketball or a day of Soccer?

74. Would you rather have an hour of Sepak Takraw or a day of Pato?

75. Would you rather have an hour of Roller Derby or a day of Caber Tossing?

76. Would you rather have an hour of bicycling or a day of skydiving

77. Would you rather have an hour of canoeing or a day of horse racing?

78. Would you rather have an hour of racing or a day of wrestling?

79. Would you rather have an hour of surfing or a day of a sausage eating contest?

80. Would you rather have an hour of skiing or a day of basketball?

Chap 11: Would You Rather - World Changers.

How would you like to help Planet Earth? What exactly would you do to help your environment or people? Pick between two helpful options in each question. You can be or do anything, you could be a legend and you can change the world!

Random:

Pick a good deed that you feel is the better option. What's more, try to put it in action after playing the game!

1. Would you rather stop using cars to minimize air pollution or start cycling to reduce air pollution?

2. Would you rather walk or use public transport to reduce air pollution?

3. Would you rather reduce the amount of food you throw away or donate to food kitchens?

4. Would you rather create compost piles or get into gardening?

5. Would you rather be eco-friendly and treasure the trees or reduce eating meat to reduce meat production and prevent factory waste pollution?

6. Would you rather stop eating dairy products or reduce your use of water?

7. Would you rather reduce paper use to save trees or use refillable water bottles and reusable lunch containers to reduce wastage and landfills?

8. Would you rather borrow or fix your clothes to stop excess production of clothes or use reusable bags to prevent pollution?

9. Would you rather print as little as necessary to help the environment or recycle?

10. Would you rather save electricity or save water, to avoid wastage?

11. Would you rather recycle glass or recycle your cellphone?

12. Would you rather recycle Aluminum or work from home to save gasoline and reduce air pollution?

13. Would you rather choose matches over lighters, to reduce the harmful junk in landfills or use paper based cotton buds to save 150 000 gallons of gasoline?

14. Would you rather use rechargeable batteries or save your notes to reduce photocopying and use of paper?

15. Would you rather spend less time in the shower to save water or share a bath with someone to reduce water wastage?

16. Would you rather plant a tree in a public park or use solar power and reduce atmospheric pollution?

17. Would you rather volunteer with a charity organization or donate something you don't use?

18. Would you rather teach people a subject you know, for a while or take a first aid course?

19. Would you rather donate money or help an elderly neighbor?

20. Would you rather use real silverware instead of plasticware or not run the dishwasher until its full?

21. Would you rather help a stressed parent to babysit or make extra snacks for your friends and/or coworkers?

22. Would you rather help a tourist find their way around the city or offer a ride to someone you know doesn't have a car?

23. Would you rather donate blood or sign up as an organ donor?

24.   Would you rather give gifts or help people out with chores?

25.   Would you rather volunteer at a community organization or at a Food Bank?

26.   Would you rather volunteer at a local hospital or help out the red cross/Salvation Army?

27.   Would you rather work in a public animal shelter or address the needs of the underprivileged or minority groups?

28.   Would you rather smile to put people in a good mood or give compliments to make people feel happier?

29.   Would you rather help a blind person cross the street or adopt a homeless pet?

30.   Would you rather help a friend achieve a goal or coach some kids to prepare them for their next games?

Careers:

What useful careers would you pick to be of service to yourself and your community? Here are a whole bunch of careers to pick from. Let's be 'career wise'!

31. Would you rather be a software developer, who works for computer firms and manufacturers, or a meteorologist, who studies the atmosphere and its phenomena?

32. Would you rather be a doctor, who treats ill or hurt people, or an airplane pilot, who controls the flight of an aircraft?

33. Would you rather be a veterinarian, who gives animals veterinary medicine or medical treatment, or an Epidemiologist, who studies diseases, causes and locations, and tries to prevent future outbreaks?

34. Would you rather be an anthropologist, who studies peoples' history and present lifestyle or a microbiologist, a scientist that studies microscopic life forms?

35. Would you rather be a medical scientist, who studies causes of diseases and other health problems, or a dentist, who treats people's teeth?

36. Would you rather be a hydrologist or a physicist?

37. Would you rather be a Dentist, and treat people teeth, or an Astronomer, a scientist who studies the fields outside the scope of Earth?

38. Would you rather be an Electrician, who installs, maintains, operates and repairs electrical equipment, or a Chemist, and be engaged in chemical research/experiments?

39. Would you rather be an Architect, who plans, designs and reviews the construction of buildings, or a Zoologist, who studies animals and their behavior?

40. Would you rather be a Mathematician, who uses his/her extensive knowledge in maths to solve mathematical problems, or a Technical Writer, who is a professional information communicator?

41. Would you rather be an Astronaut, trained to command, pilot or serve as a crew member of a spacecraft, or a Cartographer, who draws or produces maps?

42. Would you rather be a Judge, a public officer appointed to decide over cases in a law court, or a Journalist, and work in journalism to report the news?

43. Would you rather be an Accountant, who performs accounting functions, or an Artist, who paints, draws and makes sculptures?

44. Would you rather be a Builder, who constructs something by putting parts or materials together, or a Businessperson, who works in business or commerce?

45. Would you rather be a Chef, a trained, professional cook, or a Fashion Designer, who controls Fashion shows and picks models?

46. Would you rather be a Dietician, an expert on diet and nutrition, or an Economist, who is a social scientist?

47. Would you rather be a Video Game Developer, who's involved in video game development or Designing and creating games, or an Actuary, who deals with measurement and management of risk and uncertainty in business?

48. Would you rather be a Lawyer, a person who practices law, or a Police Officer, who is a warranty employee of a police force?

49. Would you rather be a Mechanic, a technician who builds, maintains or repairs machinery, or a Plumber, who supplies and repairs water pipes, baths, toilets, and so on?

50. Would you rather be a Surgeon, a physician who treats diseases, or a Cashier, who handles cash registers at his/her workplace?

Legends:

In this world there are shining stars that have changed the world for the better and these extraordinary people have become legends that will shine through history. If you could pick one, who would you prefer to be?

51. Would you rather be Eleanor Roosevelt or William Wilberforce?

52. Would you rather be Nikola Tesla or Lau Tzu?

53. Would you rather be Steve Jobs or Beethoven?

54. Would you rather be Benjamin Franklin or Ernest Hemingway?

55. Would you rather be John Lennon or George Orwell?

56. Would you rather be Genghis Kahn or Haile Selassie?

57. Would you rather be John M Keynes or Michael Faraday?

58. Would you rather be Mother Teresa or Princess Diana?

59. Would you rather be Eva Peron or Margaret Thatcher?

60. Would you rather be Martin Luther King Jr or Nelson Mandela?

61. Would you rather be Albert Einstein or Charles Darwin?

62. Would you rather be Plato or Confucius?

63. Would you rather be Sir Isaac Newton or Henry Ford?

64. Would you rather be William Shakespeare or Leonardo Da Vinci?

65. Would you rather be Rosa Parks or Marie Curie?

66. Would you rather be Malcolm X or Napoleon Bonaparte?

67. Would you rather be Christopher Columbus or Socrates?

68. Would you rather be Bill Gates or Winston Churchill?

69. Would you rather be Queen Victoria or Joan of Arc?

70. Would you rather be Galileo Galilei or Aristotle?

71. Would you rather be Leo Tolstoy or Charlemagne?

72. Would you rather be Karl Marx or Simon Bolivar?

73. Would you rather be J.S Bach or Sigmund Freud?

74. Would you rather be Muhammed Ali or Pablo Picasso?

75. Would you rather be Catherine the Great or Ataturk?

76. Would you rather be Usain Bolt or Greg Maddux?

77. Would you rather be Michael Jordan or Mike Tyson?

78. Would you rather be Manny Pacquiao or Michael Schumacher?

79. Would you rather be William Butler Yeats or Homer?

80. Would you rather be James Joyce or Robert Graves?

Bonus game: Let's find out who are all those important persons in this list! Take a computer and make some search! Who do you like the most?

Chap 12: Would You Rather - Babysitter's Trouble!

Kids are cute bundles of joy. They make us laugh and smile and are really playful and cute. Lets see what you can bear ......or can't. Pick an option that might or might not have you running to give the baby back to his/her mom.

Random:

So, what sort of kids would you prefer to handle?

1. Would you rather babysit kids that are hyperactive or one kid that loves to sing on top of their lungs?

2. Would you rather babysit a kid who loves to ruffle your hair or a kid that loves to scream into your ears?

3. Would you rather babysit a kid that talks back at you or a kid that is clingy?

4. Would you rather babysit a kid that never says thank you or never says sorry?

5. Would you rather babysit a kid that bullies siblings or a kid that breaks stuff?

6. Would you rather babysit a kid that loves watching Dora or a kid that laughs at you a lot?

7. Would you rather babysit a kid that always says no or a kid that asks the same question over and over?

8. Would you rather babysit a kid that wakes up at night to cry or a kid that never listens to you?

9. Would you rather babysit a kid that always cries for no reason or a kid that throws things at you?

10. Would you rather babysit a kid that is picky with food, or a kid that throws tantrums every five minutes?

11. Would you rather babysit a kid that throws tantrums in public or a kid that fights siblings?

12. Would you rather babysit a kid that bosses you around or a kid that doesn't share with other kids?

13. Would you rather babysit a kid that follows you everywhere or a kid that asks questions all the time?

14. Would you rather babysit a kid that doesn't listen to you or a kid that screams or shrieks all the time?

15. Would you rather babysit a kid that whines all the time or a kid that is always covered in snot?

16. Would you rather babysit a kid that can't decide what pajamas to wear, or a kid that can't decide on what food to eat?

17. Would you rather babysit a kid that watches tv all the time or a kid that watches you all the time?

18. Would you rather babysit a kid that loves to prank you, or a kid that colors the walls with crayons every time?

19. Would you rather babysit a kid that scatters the whole house or a kid that scatters the living room with paper?

20. Would you rather babysit a kid that throws things at you, or a kid that throws things at siblings?

21. Would you rather babysit a kid that is a bit disrespectful or a kid that torments the pet all the time?

22. Would you rather babysit a kid that loves to drop clothes around or a kid that drops shoes everywhere?

23. Would you rather babysit a kid that drops his/her Lego around the house all the time or a kid that drops stuffed animals everywhere?

24. Would you rather babysit a kid that pees everywhere, or a kid that wipes snot onto your clothes?

25. Would you rather babysit a kid that loves to run outside and make you run after them a lot or a kid that brings in worms and caterpillars to 'examine' them?

26. Would you rather babysit a kid that gets their way or no way or a kid that likes to pinch you for fun?

27. Would you rather babysit a kid that is super touchy or a kid that really doesn't like you?

28. Would you rather babysit a kid that loves to play with your hair or a kid that loves to pull your nose?

29. Would you rather babysit a kid that likes to kick you or a kid that is still being taught about not biting anybody?

30. Would you rather babysit a kid that wants whatever you are eating or a kid that wants whatever you have - whether its appropriate for their age or not?

Dirty Diapers:

Hopefully you don't have a phobia for changing kid's diapers, and any of their other cute but gross moments, or this section will really try you. Pick an option, or sniff a diaper!

31. Would you rather let a baby vomit into your mouth or down your new shirt?

32. Would you rather have a baby fart loudly while you change a diaper, or poop all over your hands?

33. Would you rather have a baby drool into your mouth or drool on your shirt?

34. Would you rather have a baby burp a lot or claw at your face a lot?

35. Would you rather have a baby wake you from sleep at night with crying or wake you up during an afternoon nap with crying?

36. Would you rather have a baby pee right in your face or poop right into your lap?

37. Would you rather have a baby smear your shirt with little hands covered in saliva or design your shirt with grubby hands from eating chocolate? (Either one is a great idea).

38. Would you rather have a baby pull your nose ring or pull your earring from your ear?

39. Would you rather let a baby rub saliva covered hands all over your face or stick those little hands in your ears?

40. Would you rather change a baby's diaper filled with poop, or change a baby with a pee filled diaper?
41. Would you rather let a baby try to feed you with the same toy or food they just slobbered over or throw their food on the floor in a fit?

42. Would you rather let a baby crawl all over the living room couches with cute grubby feet or mess up all your clothes with grubby hands?

43. Would you rather have a baby splash you all over with water during bath time or mess the place up with baby powder before you can snatch the powder container away?

44. Would you rather have a baby vomit all over your guests clothes while they carry him/her or barf out all the food you tried to feed them back into the plate

45. Would you rather have a baby try to poke your eyes all the time, or try to poke your nose all the time, all with wet fingers covered in baby drool? (good luck choosing an option there!)

46. Would you rather have a baby kick at your face with cute chubby feet while you carry him/her up or smack your face with their chubby little hands?

47. Would you rather have a baby slobber all over your watch or slobber all over your neck?

48. Would you rather have a baby poop right on the couch or pee on the ground?

49. Would you rather have a baby laugh and shriek really loudly when you take him/her out at a really quiet place or bang his/her rattle extra hard on your cheek?

50. Would you rather have a baby slobber all over your pens and office files, or slobber all over your car keys?

51. Would you rather have a baby take off their diaper and leave it on your work table or take off their diaper and leave it anywhere in the house?

52. Would you rather have a baby mess up all your make up and smear it on his/her face or mess up all your books and tear out a lot of pages?

53. Would you rather have a baby say 'Dada' first or have a baby say 'Mama' first?

54. Would you rather have a baby dip your clothes in water while playing or run crayons all over your homework or work files?

55. Would you rather have a baby take another babies toy (but you collect it later) or take interest in some of your own stuff (hmm) and cry all day for them?

PART TWO: TRUTH OR DARE.

It takes a great amount of emotional maturity and strength to tell the truth. While having fun, strengthen family bonds and learn a few things about each other that make everyone go 'Oooh!' or 'Aaaah!'. Something to make you blush, something to make you giggle! One embarrassing truth, another really annoying one. Warning! Some truths might not be nice at all! In no time, we'll all discover that no one is perfect... sometimes a little shock and intrigue makes life more interesting.

Instructions For The Truth or Dare Game : You might want to keep a large jug of water aside for this! Every person in the group must pick numbers and answer the questions one by one. If someone cannot answer a question, or a dare, they lose their marks or have to drink a large glass of water. If a question is answered successfully, or a dare is done, the person who answers gets five points.

- Pick those you will play the game with. No one can tell anyone outside about the truths told to the members of the game. Before and during the game, health conditions/allergies to certain activities or foods must be mentioned. Everyone should be free and loosen up, that's the point of the entire game!

Another Fun Suggestion: Everyone must take numbers and turns and each should answer the truth questions or carry their dares out. Anyone who cannot do what the dare suggests, or answer a question, will have to take two or three spoons of spicy food! Of course water should be nearby to cool the tongue of the one who backs out.

One other interesting option involves writing a few of the dares and questions on a ball and passing it to and fro. Everyone should count to ten, and then the person with the ball has to pick a question or dare and act on it. Every question answered, or dare successfully carried out, gets five marks. Good luck to all, and may the most dashing and daring win!

Truths and Dares - *Let's see how many truths you can tell, or how many dares you can take!*

1. Truth: Have you told lies about other people this year? Give it a number, and tell everyone the worst one!

OR

Dare: Pour a glass of ice cold water on your head.

2. Truth: Have you ever slept in class and gotten caught by your teacher?

OR
Dare: Go and take a bath with all your clothes on.

3. Truth: Have you taken something that isn't yours recently, and if so, what is it?

OR

Dare: Swallow a raw egg.

4. Truth: What is the silliest thing you have ever believed, that someone else told you?

OR

Dare: Go round your house jumping up and down like a frog.

5. Truth: Have you ever worn someone else's clothes and returned them before the person could see you wearing them?

OR

Dare: Wear a silly hat or glasses for the rest of the day.

6. Truth: Name two bad habits you have and always indulge in when nobody is looking.

OR

Dare: Call a friend and tell them to write whatever I say on your forehead.
7. Truth: Have you ever made a wish on a comet or wishing star?

OR

Dare: Turn round and round and pretend to chase your tail like a dog.

8. Truth: What's the thing that scares you the most? What do you do to calm yourself down every time you think of it?

OR

Dare: Sing a nursery rhyme in front of a group of people.

9. Truth: Were you ever afraid of the dark or are you still afraid of it?

OR

Dare: Go and knock a neighbour's door and tell them you love them and would love to marry them too.

10. Truth: Have you ever made a silly excuse to cover up for not doing a task? What was this excuse, if so?

OR
Dare: Tell a story that involves everyone around you and make it short. If it is not interesting and funny, you lose your points.

11. Truth: Was you/ are you ever afraid of sleeping alone?

OR

Dare: Somersault twice in an open space.

12. Truth: Are you afraid of thunderstorms?

OR

Dare: Break an egg on your head.

13. Truth: Are you afraid of clowns and why?

OR

Dare: Go without a bath for the whole of the next day.

14. Truth: What insect creeps you out the most?

OR

Dare: Try to walk backwards while dancing.

15. Truth: When was the last time you played a prank on someone and what prank did you play?

OR

Dare: Show everyone the nicest and most amazing stunt you can perform.

16.   Truth: Have you ever traded your vegetables for something else less healthy? Maybe candy or other treats?

OR

Dare: Make a nice piece of craft and complete it within thirty minutes.

17.   Truth: What movie scares you the most and/or has given you nightmares about it?
OR

Dare: Make a gross food combination and eat it.

18.   Truth: Did you ever do anything and blame it on your pet?

OR

Dare: Try to lick your elbow with your tongue.

19.   Truth: As a very young child did you ever pee on the bed and hide all the bedclothes or lie about it?

OR

Dare: Get into a staring contest with someone next to you. You win or get them some candy.

20. Truth: If you had to save someone from a natural disaster, who would you pick first?

OR

Dare: Chew five blocks of ice then take five glasses of warm water and only give five minutes of time in between.

21. Truth: Do you like cartoons and if so, who is that character that you dislike the most?

OR

Dare: Sing a love song and imitate the voice of someone you like the most.

22. Truth: Have you ever been jealous of a close friend and why?

OR

Dare: Pretend to be a statue for thirty minutes without making a single move or sound. If you do otherwise, you lose.

23. Truth: Have you ever finished chewing gum and stuck it on a surface where you thought no one would notice?

OR

Dare: Go to some random person and propose to them with a nice flower or rose.

24. Truth: Have you ever tried to run away from your shadow, or played with it, or mimicked it?

OR

Dare: Tie up your shoe laces while someone counts to ten really fast.

25. Truth: If you had to pick a different color for your eyes what would it be?

OR

Dare: Write ' I'm a goose' on your face, with lipstick. Leave to settle for twenty minutes.

26. Truth: Have you ever hidden somewhere just so you could jump out and scare someone?

OR

Dare: Say 'My mother makes me meat pies most Monday mornings' five times, very fast, without stuttering. You miss, and points are gone!

27. Truth: What's the biggest plan you have ever made to get out of chores or homework?

OR

Dare: Stay alone in a dark place for thirty minutes

28. Truth: What's the most daring thing you have ever done? Let's hear it!

OR

Dare: Remove your socks with your teeth.

29. Truth: Has a boy or girl ever embarrassed you at school? Describe that.

OR
Dare: Go next door with a measuring cup and ask for sugar.
30. Truth: Ever seen someone trip and fall in a way that made you laugh a lot? Who's that person?

OR

Dare: Pick a song and try to mime it perfectly.

31. Truth: What's the highest amount of money you have ever saved before?

OR

Dare: Lick a piece of paper, then chase someone round with it.

32. Truth: What is the most expensive thing you've ever bought, and how much did it cost?

OR
Dare: Try to balance something on your nose for five minutes.

33. Truth: Have you done something before and then put the blame on someone else?

OR

Dare: Sniff someone's armpit - then tell everyone what it smells like.

34. Truth: What's the naughtiest thing you did yesterday?

OR

Dare: Do a silly dance and then squeak like a chicken in front of a group of people.

35. Truth: Have you ever smacked or teased a pet?

OR

Dare: Get a skipping rope, then skip and count until you reach fifty. Less than fifty skips gets you less or no points.

36. Truth: Has anyone ever smacked you at school before?

OR

Dare: Spin yourself around for twenty minutes and then try to stand still without swaying.

37. Truth: Have you farted and gotten caught, while amongst a group of people, before?

Dare: Pretend to be a cat, lick your paws, and mew for thirty minutes.

38. Truth: Do you have a favorite villain from a movie and if so, name him/her.

Dare: Run up to someone and peck them twice on the cheek.

39. Truth: Have you ever had a crush on someone before? Let's know who that is.

Dare: Eat a medium sized portion of something you really don't like.

40. Truth: Have you ever tickled anyone for no reason at all?

OR

Dare: Make up your own song on the spot, sing and dance to it.

41. Truth: What's the funniest thing that's happened when you traveled?

OR

Dare: Tie a cloth as a cape and pretend you're a superhero for five minutes.

42. Truth: Do you and your best friend have a special handshake or phrase for each other?

43. Truth: Has anyone ever come to ask you to be their friend and you refused? Why?

44.   Truth: Talk about the worst trip you've ever had, and the most embarrassing things that happened.

OR

Dare: Try to pretend you are crying for a dead ant, and make it believable.

45.   Truth: What's the weirdest or funniest dream you've ever had? Describe it.

OR

Dare: Pretend to be a horse and have someone else climb on your back for a ride. For five minutes. Also try to neigh as well.

46.   Truth: Ever had a funny or embarrassing or scary moment with an animal at the zoo? Talk about it.

OR
Dare: Sing one of the songs by your favorite artiste and pretend to be them.
47.   Truth: Is there any story or movie that's ever made you cry?

OR

Dare: Take someone's smelly socks and give them a very good sniff.

48. Truth: Have you ever avoided someone because that person was really annoying?

OR

Dare: Draw your family in thirty minutes.

49. Truth: What are your best and worst colors?

OR

Dare: Pick someone to get into an arm wrestling competition with you and win. If you lose the contest, then you lose your points.

50. Truth: What animal are you scared of the most?

OR
Dare: Challenge the fastest person around you to a race and win. If you don't win, you lose your points.
51. Truth: Has an animal ever chased you around before?

OR

Dare: Try to peel a banana using your toes and no hands.

52. Truth: Have you ever peed in a swimming pool before?

OR

Dare: Wear your shoes the wrong way and show them off proudly to everyone on your street.

53. Truth: What's the most embarrassing punishment you've faced?

OR

Dare: Stand and do jumping Jacks for eight minutes.

54. Truth: What's the most embarrassing thing that has happened to you in front of your crush?

OR

Dare: Make holes for eyes in a cardboard box, wear it over your head and try to convince everyone, for thirty minutes, that you are a robot from the future. If everyone agrees that the performance is good, you get your points.

55. Truth: When was the last time you skipped your bath?

OR

Dare: Talk to a pillow like it is your best friend.

56. Truth: Have you ever forgotten to tell your best friend happy birthday?

OR

Dare: Try to jump as high as you can for thirty minutes.

57. Truth: On a day when your favorite food was prepared, have you ever eaten way too much, in a disgusting manner?

OR

Dare: Try to say ' Bunny buys butter but bakes bad buns' five times without stuttering in between your words.

58. Truth: Have you ever tried to give someone a peck on the cheek and then ran away?

OR
Dare: Eat a lot of onions and garlic and pick someone to stay close to and talk to all day.

59. Truth: Has anyone ever told you that you have body odor before?

OR

Dare: Open the front door and howl like a wolf.

60. Truth: How many times do you think of your family in a day?

OR

Dare: Run in a circle for fifteen minutes.

61. Truth: Have you ever tried to important your boss or class teacher?

OR

Dare: Take a silly picture with someone's phone.

62. Truth: Have you ever skipped brushing your teeth?

OR

Dare: Dress up as flashy as you can and catwalk like a model for your family.

63. Truth: While no one was looking, have you tried to sneak sweet treats into your bag, especially when you were told you couldn't have more?

OR

Dare: Try to balance a tray with a fruit on it on your head for thirty minutes without letting it fall.

64. Truth: Have you ever given your crush a gift?

OR

Dare: Put a pencil in your mouth and try to draw a bunch of flowers. No help with hands.

65. Truth: Have you ever hugged your crush before?

OR

Dare: Sing and pretend a brush is your microphone.

66. Truth: Have you ever left your hair messy for days on end, until it starts to smell?
OR

Dare: Balance a ball on your finger while you make your way from one end of the room to another.
67. Truth: Has anyone ever told you that your mouth smells before?

OR
Dare: Try to talk in another language.

68. Truth: Whenever you were angry with your sibling or relative, have you ever tried to do something to get them into trouble? If you did, did you apologize later?

OR

Dare: Cover your face with powder and tell everyone around that you're the 'ghost person'.

69. Truth: Have you ever eaten anything you were told not to eat and fallen ill?

OR

Dare: Brush the teeth of the person next to you.

70. Truth: When someone else was being bullied, have you ever joined in?

OR

Dare: Put a full cup of water on your head and don't allow it to fall for twenty minutes.

71. Truth: If you saw someone getting bullied by the worst bullies you know, would you run away or try to help?

OR

Dare: Go outside and dance like a cowboy.

72. Truth: Has your crush ever given you gifts before?

OR

Dare: Let someone put lipstick on your lips, and draw thick long eyebrows too.

73. Truth: Have you ever imitated someone and gotten caught before?

OR

Dare: Fill your mouth up with water and then try to sing a song.

74. Truth: Tell everyone about a show you watch that no one else knows about?

OR

Dare: Balance a stick on one finger for ten seconds without letting it fall off.
75. Truth: Have you ever pooped in your pants before?

OR
Dare: Let someone do some make up on your face for you.

76. Truth: Have you ever played a prank on someone else by putting insects or worms in their clothes or food?

77. Truth: How many times have you dreamt of your crush (spouse)?

OR
Dare: Give a tree in your back yard a quick hug.

78. Truth: Do you actually care about dressing up nicely or you just do it so nobody can complain about you?

OR

Dare: Mix up two different food items in a weird combination and eat them.

79. Truth: Have you been mean to a pet while no one was looking?

OR

Dare: Eat half of a lemon without making faces.
80. Truth: Do you clean your environment or room often or only when you know someone might scold you?

OR

Dare: Crawl round everyone in a circle.

81. Truth: Have you ever cut an insect into pieces while it was alive or burnt one with a matchstick?

OR

Dare: Try to balance on your toes like a ballerina for ten minutes.

82. Truth: Has anyone successfully gotten to scare you through a prank before?

OR

Dare: Get an item and try to sell it to everyone as if you are a salesperson.

83. Truth: Ever tried to mix up nonsense pretending that you were experimenting with chemicals?

84. Truth: Have you ever been in front of your crush and been unable to speak or just said some nonsense words?
85. Truth: Have you ever TOTALLY FORGOTTEN to brush your teeth?

OR

Dare: Arm wrestle with someone else.

86. Truth: Do you still like teddy bears and toys and dolls?

87. Truth: During lunch time at school, have you ever shared food with your crush?

88. Truth: Are you good at video games or just lousy?

OR

Dare: Stand up and mimic a parent or another older person.

89. Truth: Are you confident enough to walk up to a stranger and tell them that you like them?

90. Truth: Have you ever tried to cook or bake something and it turned out terrible?

91. Truth: Have you tried to exchange lunches with someone else before? What was the worst exchange?

92. Truth: Have you ever been so scared that you peed in your pants before?

OR

Dare: Toe wrestle with someone else.

93. Truth: Have you ever been so angry that you broke something out of anger?

94. Truth: When you really liked someone, have you sent an anonymous love letter to them?

95. Truth: Would you freak out if you had to hold a living, squeaking, fierce chicken?

OR

Dare: Walk round everyone telling them 'Good day ma'am, good day sir, would you like a smelly onion?'

96. Truth: Have you ever dressed up as something scary just to scare someone?

OR

Dare: Go and tell a neighbour ' Welcome to the neighborhood!'.

97. Truth: Have you ever blown a kiss to someone before?

OR

Dare: Do ten sit ups and ten push-ups.

98. Truth: Do you often look into the mirror and admire yourself, like, a lot?

OR

Dare: Hold the hand of the person next to you for thirty minutes and stare at the person intently.

99.   Truth: Have you ever laughed at someone that everyone else was laughing at?

OR

Dare: Put on your clothes from the inside out.

100.   Truth: If you used the bathroom and discovered there was no toilet paper to clean up, what would you do?

OR

Dare: Talk to someone like they're your pet.